THE WALL DANCER

Previous collections by Alan Dixon:

Snails and Reliquaries (The Fortune Press)
The Upright Position (Poet & Printer)
The Egotistical Decline (Poet & Printer)
The Immaculate Magpies (Poet & Printer)
The Hogweed Lass (Poet & Printer)
A Far-Off Sound (Poet & Printer)
Transports (Redbeck Press)
The Ogling of Lady Luck (Shoestring Press)
The Seaweed's Secret (After Max Jacob) (Spectacular Diseases)
73 Woodcuts (Shoestring Press)

All rights reserved. No part of this work covered by the copyright herein may be reproduced or used in any means – graphic, electronic, or mechanical, including copying, recording, taping, or information storage and retrieval systems – without written permission of the publisher.

Printed by imprintdigital
Upton Pyne, Exeter
www.digital.imprint.co.uk

Typesetting and cover design by narrator
www.narrator.me.uk
info@narrator.me.uk
033 022 300 39

Published by Shoestring Press
19 Devonshire Avenue, Beeston, Nottingham, NG9 1BS
(0115) 925 1827
www.shoestringpress.co.uk

First published 2017
© Copyright: Alan Dixon

The moral right of the author has been asserted.

ISBN 978-1-910323-96-0

THE WALL DANCER

ALAN DIXON

ACKNOWLEDGEMENTS

Acknowledgements are due to the following, in which some of these poems appeared: *Ambit, Carillon, Cat Kist* (The Redbeck Anthology of Contemporary Cats), *Chanticleer Magazine, The Dark Horse, 14 Magazine, The Frogmore Papers, The Journal, Moodswing, The North, Orbis, Pennine Platform, Poetry Scotland, The Projectionist's Playground, The Rialto, Smiths Knoll, Smoke, The Spectator, Stand, The Times Literary Supplement.*

CONTENTS

Village	1
Road Walker	2
A Granite Armchair	3
Evidence	4
The Naked Man at Poverty Bottom	5
Wounded Gull	6
Seven Crows Hanging	7
Lost Juvenilia	8
Swedenborg Complete	9
Out of Green Doglick Jumped the Humpy Snail	10
Don Quixote's Letterbox	11
At the Archaeological Museum, Naples	12
Ragbo!	13
Blue, Blue-Black, Grey-Black and True Black	14
Thirtyfivers	15
The Wolf Whistle	16
If You Forget	17
A Mouse	18
A Dogfish	19
The Window-Hoverer	20
Cock	21
To Bardsey Island and Back	23
Jackdaws	24
A Quarter of Cockles	25
Time to Lock Up	26
At the Torino Café	27
Sunday Painter	28
First Term, 1959	29
A Hat for the Group Show Opening	30
Archilochos the Hoplite	31
Museum of Allotments	32
Worlds	33
The Old Violin Mender	34
The Horse-Husband	35
The Old Upright in the Chinese Takeaway is Waiting for this Notice	36

The Chocolate Gentleman	37
Cubism	38
Heatwave of 1912, Berlin	39
Campendonk	40
Eulogy	41
Tumult	42
The Wall Dancer	43
To My Brother	44
An Engineer's Reserve	45
Back from Death Again	46
An Everyman	47
The Bolster	48
At the Cross Keys	49
Diademas Extra	50
The Bustards	51
The Stationmaster	52
Smoky Sailor	53
The Coalman	55
Two Guides	56
Hesitation	57
Dissatisfied Jack	58
A Useful Meeting	60
Remembering W Price Turner	61
Full Moon at St Seine L'Abbaye, 1906	62
Max Beerbohm and the Lark	63
Fastidious Smith	64
Pirate Pencil	65
Fatshirt's Prescription	66
King Ubu's Bath	67
The Juggler	68
Dobbo the Roofman	69
Drill Instructor's Dinner	70
A Freckled Visitor	71
Rhyme of the Scribbler's Mother	72
Episode at Halifax	74
Young Beggar in Andalusia	75
In Rotterdam	76
By the Fisherman's Hut	77
The Shepherds	79

Clara Greylees	80
The Fountain Girl	81
Smoke	82
The Snake Hole	83
Her Shoes	84

VILLAGE

Slams and quarrelsome knocks, bleats and a moo or two;
A famished man with sodden socks, a heel-less shoe;
A dragging dragon yapping at a coppery cockadoodledoo.

A wet frock in leaves, whose body has gone
Somewhere unknown to the mother and everyone,
Waits, wets, dries, is rained on again.

A wayfarer enters the village and comes to the inn.
One for the fashion he has scratched and nettled his shin and
    stubbled his chin.
He sits in the garden in sunlight to be seen
Reading motoring magazine after motoring magazine.

A sycamore sapling waving one leaf like a frantic hand.
A squeezed branch creaking in what little is left of a wind.

ROAD WALKER

Between the traffic and the falling wall,
Between the swamp and overtaking vans
Batting to hell and thumping as they go
Something called music, cutlery and pans,
The poor pedestrian (must be if he must crawl
The pot-holed line), too delicate to know
The thrill of rabbit squashing, sees big dogs
Grinning from windows, wanting to escape
Prestigious cages, even on a rope.

The fizz no longer bubbles in his brain,
Nor need he lift his head at beep or shout.
All vehicles are ugly but those with snout
In memory of horses. Road hogs strain
Braces and tempers, name unfair to pigs.

A GRANITE ARMCHAIR

There is a granite armchair
In County Galway, somewhere
Men did not choose;
But I could not sit there,
For when I passed beside,
Walking along the road,
It was already occupied
By a leisurely man who did not look
Prepared to take
His arse off for a stranger's sake;
And by him others were meeting
Who thought granitic seating
Was not for me, were estimating
Unsuitability as I passed,
Turning their igneous heads as I walked west.

EVIDENCE

    Across the path
    A walking-stick
    And further on
A bandage and a pad.

    So what do you
    Surmise of them?
    Is this the way
A miracle has gone?

    How far behind
    The limping then
    The leaping one
Unloading ache and pain?

THE NAKED MAN AT POVERTY BOTTOM

Do you remember the naked man at Poverty Bottom?
You noticed him first, in his garden, I only caught a glimpse.
You were sniffing one of his yellow roses by the gate
And I was looking up at the swallows on the wires.

Did the bullaces we gathered for jam remind you of his bottom?
We couldn't be bothered to stone them all, just gave them a rinse.
It must have been sometime in June. I made a note of the date:
To return for three if not four, with the boxes the fruit requires.

Was it that year the horsewoman suddenly came upon us
As we sat down for our Stilton sandwiches on a grassy patch?
She didn't approve of that; she even accused us of hiding.
It had never happened to her before when she was riding.
The horse had thundered off and wasn't easy to catch.
Though the shape of the bottom was boiled was it all in the
    jam like a bonus?

WOUNDED GULL

Since my old friend, forty years lost, now lost again,
Said I should not try to help the gull thrashing against the rock-fall
– As if he'd known me as one who sought and took his advice –
And since I held it and folded it in my hands so easily, and he'd
    been able
Easily to show no surprise at a success he didn't expect or approve,
At how it did not peck but seemed to know I tried to help
As I carried it beyond rocks to a sandy part of the beach,
And reached from a lapped stone as far as I could
And dropped it onto the sea where it swam not far from the others,
Where it would have a chance, if it could not fly properly,
And since he too looked back, his only politeness about it, to
    see how it balanced,
I have loved the ebullient brown-headed black-headed gulls,
The buoyant squealers who cross their wingtips high, out of
    the reach of the waves,
And I have hoped that wounded one is somewhere alive,
    and mended.

SEVEN CROWS HANGING

Wings tied with frayed string, crows hang in a row,
　Hang on a barbed wire, pronged feet brushed by green
In wind from the sea, as food for the blow-
　fly shrivelled and frayed; wings raggedly fan.

Thin bones swing together, claw feather and beak.
The blue of their gloss flew back to the sky.
Dry rhombic throat skins drag on bands of stretched neck.
Thrown flight and bright black have helped them to die.

Can crows be bleached white? How long could they hang?
As long as the knots hold bits of frayed string
And posts hold the wire there'll be some bones to show
Of seven shot crows that hang in a row.

LOST JUVENILIA

Flowers of youth squeezed in secret black notebooks,
Mockery of maths on square-ruled paper,
Locked in a trunk, now lost forever,
Rocks bones and toads in miraculous junctures.

Black ink he used and black ink always;
Each was tossed off with his lack of logic,
And he would cover if anyone entered.

He clutched at the crest of the horse as it galloped,
Sometimes holding, sometimes flung
Into a cowpat or patch of thistle.

Could he recover that shamefaced freedom
A child of today would present to his mentor?
Now he is sure he would listen astonished
To the youth he murdered for space and correction,
Who gathered blooms as the horse flew on,
Who ate and drank on a cantering table.

SWEDENBORG COMPLETE

On routine inspections even the pacing-stick poker
Had nothing to say about the books in my locker:
Collected Yeats and Thomas, the Sesame Book
Of Ezra Pound, selected, I guess, by Possum.
I even had The Cantos, a hefty volume,
And later (God help me!) for understanding Blake,
Swedenborg complete, which I never read.
(I swallowed the wild and windy Welshman instead.)
I couldn't have paid a lot for that sizeable packet.
I saw the sultry girl that bulky day.
As I left the astonished shop I whisked her away.
So dreamt a scruffy conscript with one tweed jacket,
One pair of shoes, although those shoes were leather
And good enough for two lost years of Hampshire weather.

OUT OF GREEN DOGLICK JUMPED THE HUMPY SNAIL

Out of green doglick jumped the humpy snail.
A saw-scraped husk and octopus of lead
Hoisted October on Cadaver's whale
With horn and dishrag on·his drum-tapped head
Or swish of spume or teeth in donkey's brine
Where dunking ponds unshine.

Twist on the limbs of lobsters in the flash
Of grizzled wigs and canticles of spot
Where bruises blind stagged mandrakes waxed with cash
And spigots pick a thundertaker's trot.
Clipped out of cloudlings Adam thumbs his nose
And hard-held hopes repose.

Augustus-brushed, a crosser of the noughts,
Dumpily daft in dazzle camouflage,
Bombastifies sloshed sailors in black ports
Where whopping women weep for cocks at large.
Webbed kitchen crones from creaky cupboards leap
And cocklescratchers creep.

A pompous fog hops off across the docks
Mopping the figleaf on the wooden maid,
Puffing the hands and legs of owling clocks,
Pickling the rib of love in lemonade
Under a smokelit moon of mitching sponge
Where spankers snap and lunge.

Lankly the catfish threads a treble clef
Through burning baskets stuffed with bubbling drunks
Where backward hatchets pulverize the chef
With lumpy echoes, crocodilic clunks
And rhubarb men in scissored stockings cough
Their laughing scallops off.

DON QUIXOTE'S LETTERBOX

Dear Don Quixote, I have looked for your letterbox
Knowing I'd recognise it instantly.
I have not only a message of sympathy,
But I, Don Dixote, believe myself a poet
And climb on my tall horse skinny as we are
To issue words to next to nobody
Which once I believed made sense to anybody,
Not only cranks.

          I have no Dulcinea
Or squire to justify futility
But in my quest for your rusty iron letterbox
My horse of fancy lifts me bonily.

The box must bear resemblance to your helmet.
I hope I shall be posting to please your mad
Old brain, as if a helmet means a head.

AT THE ARCHAEOLOGICAL MUSEUM, NAPLES

Those marble emperors, so many, so white,
The colossal one, Vespasian probably,
Head cut off flat at the top
So you could sit up there
And dangle your feet by his nose
Or post a note
In the imperial mouth most right for that:

Tell me about yourself, briefly.
You can't have been such a blockhead.
What do you think of all this immortalized waiting,
Not even what we call waiting about?
Tell him you'll remember best
A pot frog,
The mosaic ducks and dog.

RAGBO!

Ragbo! shouted the ragman in those days,
His old cart rumbling near and rattling by,
A hazardous entanglement piled high
With unsprung mattresses and banging trays
And iron bedsteads which complained the most;
Few rags, and never bones that I could see.
Loosely he held the rein against his knee;
He looked to us as drab as trodden toast
On a winter pavement black with dropping fog.

But high up on the mattresses reposed,
Dreaming of that rare thing a toothsome bone,
A little yapping type of happy dog
Who, nose low, through all the commotion dozed.
It took the worst of jolts to make him moan.

BLUE, BLUE-BLACK, GREY-BLACK AND TRUE BLACK

Ten guineas a term, one for each inky finger.
A tinny teapot for the blue-black ink.
Exercises reversed on blotting paper.
Blue Pocket Oxford – huge for a pocket book.
Mr Smith, headmaster, whose Christian name
We never knew; his mortarboard had no
Mortar on it ever, and no flame
Burned underneath his sooty gown to show
To boys of eight or nine. Old Wadnesford,
Protected only by his blacker gown,
Stressing the middle syllable of the word,
Told us his name. He wore no mortarboard.
He didn't laugh at baskets toppling down
With crumpled paper on his grey-black head.

THIRTYFIVERS

You could hear them coming, their blakeys and segs,
Croaky bells on their grids and bulby tooters.
There were hawkers and spitters, mostly in gutters.
Shorts were for shrimps: they were quick to cover their legs.
Most of them didn't have muscly ones: there wasn't much to carry.
To be sure of some shagging they expected to marry
And those who didn't or hadn't didn't want any.
In those neo-romantic days even the most cherubic
Choirboys remained telluric.
Haircream and chewing gum made them sticky.
They liked the back row at the flicks and they were flicky
With the bugrakes in their top pockets.
Some were adept at crackling their knuckle sockets.
The tops of their ears had a place for a piece of a pencil.
For calculations a lick of the lead was essential.
There were no superstitious advantages for crosses or noughts.
'Satisfactory' was good enough, for them, on school reports.
They were fonder of the stench
Of boiling glue than French.
Most wore braces but the toughest were strapped with a buckle.
Their roller skates made a tremendous chuckle.
When they upset their mas they knew no apple carts, only go-carters.
They had either floppy socks or ferocious garters.
New studs were hammered onto footer boot soles
Successfully if they trod on the nails.
It was best to leave the field statuesque with mud,
With no need to knife any grass from round a stud.
Winners and losers, wind sticking their baggy sails
Trudged off to scraping grinding squeaking nails
With quiffs knocked about and sparks in their trails.
The most admired was the bright spark,
The best inventor of the lark.

THE WOLF WHISTLE

The wolf whistle fizzled
Away in wind with the whistling habit.
It could be squeezed by any buck-toothed rabbit.
We were not wolves who whistled
This augmentation of birdsong
When days grew long
Again and we could see how silky
Girls were as well as sulky.

O wolf whistle come
Back to show admiration of these slim
Long legs, these not-too-dumpy, these medium…
Return for boys who wish to whistle and some
Unbrazen girls whose subtle
Beauty should be witnessed with a whistle,
For girls who want to know.
Few blew for nothing. Blow, whistlers! Blow!

IF YOU FORGET

If you forget I want to be burned
To cinders you can cut me in two
And cram me in a small child's grave,
Give me a stone without a name
– Just my initials A M D,
Or M A D if you think I'm mad –
A boulder for a collared dove
To perch on purring, folding its fan;
Plant marigolds or any flower
That grows as easily as weed,
A toadstool with a copper top
As a reminder of my head,
And whirligigs, beetle and wasp,
So all can see I died a child
And I can grin about the lie.

A MOUSE

Here is a muscular mouse
Creeping over your bones,
In and out of the cage,
Over the keyboard of spine
Patting a scratch of a tune,
Putting his nose in your nose,
Peeping around in your eyes.
Still you have eyes of a kind.
If there is seeing beyond
He'll do the seeing for you.
Haven't you felt his tail
Trailing your shivery skin?
He is your afterlife
Scratching the itch on your head,
Even replacing your nose
– Always a troublesome thing.
You can believe in him.

A DOGFISH

Some days I want a dogfish of my own.
I'm in the mood for a low-down grumpy glare.
At other times a catfish or a square
Juan Miró fish, fanned canvases on bone.

You might mistake it for my freckled arm
Except it has an opening underneath
The elbow, and my elbow has no teeth
Unless it breaks to make a jagged crack.

I wouldn't break an arm for friendship's sake
Or say my hand and fishtail look the same,
Though I could imitate its spotty sweep.

For tanks the black-mouthed dogfish swims too deep.
It is the spotted I am thinking of.
The spur-dog is a tricky fish to love.

THE WINDOW-HOVERER

What happened to that woman-botherer,
That owlish fowl the window-hoverer?

Its stare could pierce through steam but strained to pass
Round curtains and through pinkened frosted glass.

Few birders watched it pecking at the panes
Of bathing ladies, buffeting its brains.

Some called it the pane-pecker. Shooting was not
Advisable. Who wants their windows shot?

Its whiskered squinty look was rediscovered
When a meaning laugh was heard in a bathroom cupboard.

Never protected; no one took its part;
It wasn't nice enough to move the heart.

Dangle its semblance from a lifted pole
At saturnalia and carnival.

COCK

Whatever the dictionaries tell us, who's prepared to talk about a
    cock any more?
Even the effers and blinders have to call it a cockerel.
Should I feel sorry for fierce old and splendid mature cocks for
    being so diminished?
They look cocky as ever to me.
Is it like being called young man by those no older than I am?
And how could anyone feel cockerel-a-hoop about it?
But it doesn't look like a cock-up to the cockerel people;
They're not afraid to talk about a cock which isn't a cock;
They don't turn the water off at the stop-cockerel,
Though a few of them might blush or grin at the mention of a
    weathercock or a soldier with a cockade or a visit to
    Cockfosters.
(It ought to give a bit of a booster to the word rooster.)

Is it all a plan to aggrandize the penis,
To make it seem loud and feathered and brave?...
May the true cocks take revenge on their usurpers and peck
    them to noodly ribbons.
Cocks, I insist on continuing to call you cocks;
Spare me at your reckoning time.
No wonder one of you is forcing the irate people of Peveril
    Road to close their windows and wear earplugs.
This is only the beginning.

I've seen it. It looks like a cock to me,
And they're the kind of people to call a spade a spade
And a mere penis couldn't flap up into a bush, which could be
    a tree, and make such a racket and wouldn't be hard to catch,
Nor would a man in Castor Mrs Someone knows (she has his
    number) want it for his hens.
Perhaps in Castor they call a cock a cock, and a cockerel is
    only a youngster, and a cock has its place,

Though I don't think it's only townspeople who feel shy of the word.
Nearly everybody for miles around is a natural exaggerator
    who claims to face the facts,
But that a cock is a cock is too much for them all.

TO BARDSEY ISLAND AND BACK

I'm chuffed to see the choughs at last
But came back waxing black as one:
Smuts speckling the exhaust stuck on
The taker of the smoky seat
In Captain Pritchard's risky boat.

She chugged across the choppy sound,
Left Aberdaron smudged to lee.
His bags were rolled above the knee.
Silk rags took fire. The ciao of choughs
Greeted me from the monkish cliffs.

JACKDAWS

Happy the jackdaws surrounded by their playmate
Boisterous wind with which they wrestle and roll,
Diving against it, wings closed; gripped and thrown
Many ways, open-winged, spun in it chacking and looping.

Easy to envy jackdaws. Even those
Who never look up, who curse the stopped and creeping
Traffic must see their low flight in the distance
As they descend to towns jackdaws poke fun at,
See them in swirling pairs, amused and mated
For life, defeated only when no one knows
And never bullied by a wind too gusty.

Having lived too long in a town no jackdaw trusted,
Whose graveyards lacked their disrespectful tread,
I spend my careless time airing my head.

A QUARTER OF COCKLES

I have a quarter of cockles to share
With old tabby Cedric, my tangled cat.
After each cockle I make him stare,
Look lively as so long before
He became a shadowy bag of sharp bone.

He tells me he wants to live forever
If there are cockles, not mind the comb
Any more than vinegar, salt and pepper.
Tithonus was lonely. He had no pet.
Old scrap, I hope we can shrink together.

TIME TO LOCK UP

Where's my cat Dapple
Stalking or squatting
On freckled legs?
Not where the rain
Shines on the flags
In kitchen light.
Is she in shelter
Watching it dropping
From leaf to pebble?

No cry to tell us
Till out of hiding
Through the yellow
Corydalis
She comes sliding
On cold wet feet,
Slugs in the gaps
Between her pads,
Shunning a wiping.

AT THE TORINO CAFÉ

What's taking Whistler's side to do
With bacon, liver, onions, beans
And homemade bubble and squeak, well scorched
In a former Italian restaurant?

I see a blue plaque opposite
Beside a grim black iron gate:
The residence of Samuel Prout,
Ruskin, but Sickert too, admired.

I could have just walked by (and did
First time) not knowing, as if lost
In a Whistlerian crépuscule,
A figure blobbed against a shop.

This liver would not taste the same
If I had thought Whistler to blame
And favoured Ruskin's argument,
The armoured finish of Burne-Jones,

Not seen the girl with the chunk of cheese
Soft in her hand rubbed over blades,
And watched it pile and brim the dish
Till I felt steel across my palm.

SUNDAY PAINTER

He paints on Tuesday, Saturday, any day.
Up in his loft Sundays are any day
Except the coldest. When the days are hot
He lifts the window, makes the gulls complain.
A hole in the roof! The roof is their domain.
He often thinks one might jump in or fall,
Pick up a brush and give a tube a peck.

He hopes his finished pictures tell him what
Title to paint in capitals on the back.
– But not in black, he's running out of black.
He wishes he could train the boldest gull,
Emma, to fly to town with cash in beak
– She often flies to town and back – fly back
With oil paint tubes, starting with ivory black.

FIRST TERM, 1959

They tossed their brushes high and gave him a Pollock ceiling.
The window cleaners stamped cleats on the drying pictures.
The lock on the door straight into the playground was easy to break
So they broke it often, in play, and turned up the tables and chairs
Which kicked their legs in the air and laughed.
He tied the doorknob to a radiator with a rope
And when that frayed he tied it with another.

From one window he could see the other sex playing netball,
And Bedlam just behind,.or the site of it,
Where meths drinkers reclined on grass.
The boys painted little square vans with METH on the sides.

That Christmas he had lots of presents,
So many cigars, though no one had seen him smoking,
And classes of fifty in the state of emergency.
The headmaster pulled up his shirtsleeves with bands
And painted art nouveau peacocks on the panto backdrop,
Had done the same sort of thing every December
And wanted neither comment nor assistance.

A HAT FOR THE GROUP SHOW OPENING

Her old father, persuaded to wear an artist's hat
Over his artist's hair, though she not he was the artist,
Found it, when not on his head, a bother to carry about.
Was he independent enough to think of tossing it out
Through the wide-open window, spinning it into the park?

He handed it to the ad hoc barman (who was giving
A lecture, prompted by the newly-acquired John Lake,
El Disfraz, to an Ernst enthusiast with a blank
Where the British Surrealists ought to be), asked him to look
After it carefully, not sit on or try on or spill on or sell it.

Somehow he bought the drinks without opening his wallet
Or purse or delving in his pocket. How could the hat,
The mere presence of it, be a substitute for payment?
She thought it enhanced her reputation quite a lot.

ARCHILOCHOS THE HOPLITE

Walking through winter woods with my sharp spade
Why do I think of Archilochos the hoplite?
Do I bring perturbation to old ladies toddling
Dogs whose little teeth could not bite through
Wellingtons, thick trousers and muddy waterproof?
In his campaign in Thasos he must have frightened
Peachy shepherdesses and whited wheezers.
I shall never couple urgently in these woods
In the ripping brambles beside the dogshitty paths.
Was it prickly pasture for Archilochos the hoplite?
Was it orchids and asphodel he pressed them down on?
I can hardly imagine him putting aside his spear
As 'his dong flooded over like a stall-fed donkey's',
Or having patience enough to reach his sixties.
Our service was wasted time. There were no spoils.
He would have scorned air marshals, if he'd seen them,
For not being like his stumpy bowlegged general.

MUSEUM OF ALLOTMENTS

Vincent might have painted
These gardening gloves
Like the muddy old boots
The pile of spuds.

Black-shined and holey
Relics of toil
From the Museum of Allotments,
A tourist pull.

Shove some junk together,
Charge entrance, serve tea,
Behind a glass wall
Stuffed dunnock, stuffed me;

Stuffed Norman Mucklin
In the actual shed
Where he poked an old flame
– The lucky lad;

The strip of a skirt
Torn off on a rust-
y nail on a fence
When her scratch was kissed;

The willow klompen
The wag would wear;
A green finger
To give you a scare.

WORLDS

Your world, my world, his world: world's the new word.
These little fragments made whole and big with purpose,
Planets with polished nights, bright lights, each
Not a neck of the woods any longer, more than a life,
Centres, Romes, radiations, so many big cheeses.

Some of us scratch on hills, not knowing how far
Worms go down, their up, in the skin of the world;
Or in the valley you listen to rain in the night,
Wishing you lived on the water, a Tang drunkard,
The world lifting you, and you subsiding with it.

THE OLD VIOLIN MENDER

His room was cramped and poor, the instruments
Hung their rococo shadows everywhere.
I left my fiddle with him for repair
But took the box and its accoutrements
Back up the hill to home wishing I had
A proper waisted case, though that black coffin
Was big enough to put my extra stuff in:
Music and towel and trunks – must have been mad.

But still the sponge my mother had to bake
On hearing my description of the place
Would not fit, even in the empty case
When I returned with it, and balanced cake.

Some Lambeth tailor, squatting in the gloom
Of mother's memory, had shared the room.

THE HORSE-HUSBAND

We know the horse puffing a thoughtful pipe
Shows at her dusty window late at night
Smoking his own dry dung, nosing the pane.
His heap of straw was once a fiery mane.

She teaches violin to little boys.
Each tail strand feels the upstroke and the down.
She used to stroke his skin of fiddle brown
And take his tuning peg and twist it tight.

He knocks and scrapes his pipe and clops to bed.
She switches on a skirt of yellow light
By which the horse had read his Sherlock Holmes,
His Speckled Band. He tamps his bedtime crumbs.

She patches sheets his hoof so often tears.
She sniffs knife-handle scorch; his match heads shine
Like fireflies in the ash. She never dares
Replace his broken cup of blackened bone.

THE OLD UPRIGHT IN THE CHINESE TAKEAWAY IS WAITING FOR THIS NOTICE

Lang Lang play here
And take away.
He did not pay.
We did not let
After all that.
With no menu
He play Liszt.
This old wood thing
You put food on
And make a ring,
He make it go,
He make it sing,
He make it bang
With special bang,
Bang of Lang Lang.
How do he do?
The wood it know.
We ask it to
Remember. Though
It show no lack
It want him back
To play again,
The best of all
Piano men,
The best to sing,
The best to bang.

THE CHOCOLATE GENTLEMAN

Erik Satie
Liked a bar of chocolate.
If not does it matter
Now he has gone?

In all his list
Of works for piano,
Solo or duo,
There's no chocolate one.

If he liked chocolate
As much as I do
His Pièces de chocolat
Would be several bars long.

I see him in
A snappy brown velvet
Suit of squares
Embossed or indented.

If you compose
Make up with a Morceau
Of parody Satie
Pour le piano

En forme de lapin
Wobbly and cold,
Chocolate blancmange
From a glass mould.

CUBISM

When Francis Picabia said
Cubism is a cathedral of shit
He meant the analytic bit,
But when it changed, got rid
Of the doctrinaire and wiped
Its arse, brought out washed flags,
Striped bathing costumes, circuses,
Bands, dotty cloths and sandwich men
Who did not forecast doom some said
It had been much misunderstood,
Had no right, with the First World War
And so on, to be glad.

HEATWAVE OF 1912, BERLIN

Some nights I, Ludwig Meider, must
Go to the city, tugged, my stride
Stretches towards the centre, soon
I hustle along the pavements. Screams
Of cloud echo around my head.
Bushes in flames. A distant beat
Of wings. The shadowy people spit.
The moon is burning against my hot
Temples as the city nears
And swells to me. My body cracks
And crackles. The city's sniggers ignite
My skin. At my skull's base I hear
Eruptions as apartments loom
And sway to me. Catastrophes
Explode from windows, stairs collapse
Silently as the people laugh
Beneath the ruins. On I step.
I dare not stop for anything.

CAMPENDONK

(After Franz Richard Behrens)

Pointed leaves
Dances
Bouquets
Grain shading
Rib ring
Forest wandering
Lost sungold
Pearled wineblood
Twirled
Suspended
Darted
Pinecone grenade
Arrowed shooting star
Sun drinks bloodcup
Cricket husk red breeze
Lake mussel curve
Blue leafboats
Blue blood bubbles
Violet sunfloor green shells
Rucked tigerrug
Kobaldblue comet reins
Notched streets leap
Toothed tunnel leaps
Thirst leaps peeping through
Snow wine star wave
Snakebirth spring dragging banners
Armoured pipes bloodcollar kraterheat
Dagger eyes tongues
Horserams
Trembling wave world.

EULOGY

(After Jakob van Hoddis)

Bladdy Groth
Was a girl of gentle blood,
Bladdy Groth, Bladdy Groth is dead.
Bladdy Groth was a girl of tender blood
And she was kind to men both good and bad
And none had a spirit so free and glad.
Bladdy Groth, Bladdy Groth, Bladdy Groth.

And she sang and she played and danced through the night
And she laughed at me and was high as a kite.
Bladdy Groth, Bladdy Groth is dead.

And for everyone she had no affectation
And that includes the useless one I mention.
Bladdy Groth, Bladdy Groth, Bladdy Groth.

And her neck, it was for burning kisses
And for no one had she any defences.
Bladdy Groth, Bladdy Groth, Bladdy Groth.

And her eyes shot lightning's blue
And her dresses were mostly heaven-blue.
Bladdy Groth, Bladdy Groth, Bladdy Groth.

Ah, how can cock-winged Lucifer stand her
As she flutters in her angel's paraphernalia?
Bladdy Groth, Bladdy Groth!
What Sekt is uncorked high up in heaven
Now she is an angel woman?

TUMULT

(After Max Jacob)

Tumult of horses, warring Mikado
Honeysuckle on a golden ground
It could be a gift
From my latest Romeo
It hangs on my wrist
He loves me with amazement
Viol, viola, violin, I am ultraviolet
I leave for Chicago
I am dying in the compartment.

THE WALL DANCER

My brother, who was boss, being three years older,
And I were persuaded to go on a week-long wander
With Mother's lover's boy – with the inhaler –
Over hills and dales, my brother the map reader
Who pointed the way, but made neither big talk nor small.

We must have been lucky lads one day with the weather;
We were lounging against a wobbly wall when the intruder
Climbed up and started to dance and kicked a boulder
– Limestone? or millstone grit? I can't remember –
Onto my brother's head, but it didn't matter
To the hero: he never complained with his back to a wall.

I thought for one terrible moment that he was a goner
Till he gave me a look which was less than the shrug of a shoulder.
His wiry hair, unturned, had cushioned the fall.

TO MY BROTHER

What a buffoon I used to be!
Still am! Remember those cycling shoes,
Ginger, like both you and me,
And never a pair I'd want to lose,

And that day I got them soaked in France
And put them in the top of a stove
To dry overnight. You'd have more sense,
Though I wonder my foolishness didn't move

You to use it then. When I took them out
They were shrivelled and scorched and far too small
To put on my feet, and looked like what?
– Kippers perhaps; no use at all.

So I had to go in stockinged feet
To buy some ridiculous espadrilles
Which were all I could afford and not
Much use for pedalling up the hills

Or down the hills. I never had
Such beautiful shoes again to fit
Into my clips. I think it sad
You didn't have time to cure me of it

– That foolishness. I'm sure the heels
Dragged in the road and scraped the dust,
But I must have managed to push the wheels....
What good reminding the dead, the lost!

How much difference you might have made
After the silence of your reproof.
I couldn't have been as sharp as a blade.
I mightn't have been such a careless oaf.

AN ENGINEER'S RESERVE

When my brother decided to sign on for three years
Did Colonel W R Swale, headmaster, advise him
To choose the Engineers because of his temperament?

A note in 'In Parenthesis' mentions that mystery of theirs,
How Engineers seemed always to be up to some job
About which they maintained an irritating reserve.

I met my brother only once in those years.
He was in uniform, as if he had found his life,
Though his letters had said nothing and he was due for demob.

I wasn't a proper airman and the army was different.
We tried to make our working blues last the full two years.
Out of camp even the regulars wore civvies.

In a letter to him I had copied 'Byzantium',
Though I made no claim to an understanding of it.
I'm sure he approved of my first seriousness.

That day he had the keenness and colour of mustard.
I can't think why he didn't sign on for longer.
And when he was alive I didn't ask him.

It's the same with death as with Egypt: I'd like to know more.
Are there free travel passes? Is it a cushy number?
Is it best for the regulars, the serious people?

BACK FROM DEATH AGAIN

My brother, back from death again – how does he do it?
Wearing a long bright turquoise gabardine he's running
Up the steps and the old garden path to the back door.
I rush to him. Who left an insole on the floor,
    Or a white shoeprint?

He's here so noiselessly the door must have been open.
The scientists, he says, keep asking to be paid.
Surely he comes to console and not to ask for money
Or to explain. His endearments had to be understood,
    Could not be spoken.

AN EVERYMAN

Naked myself I carried my dead
Naked brother on my back
For days. We went about on foot,
By bus and train. So little weight!
He had become so dry and black.

One man was curious enough
To ask what I was reading, and
His name. I read an Everyman.
I told the man his name was John.
A name for everyman, he said.

THE BOLSTER

Between me and my brother lay the bolster.
With what was it filled? It wasn't stuffed with feather;
Nothing so natural, not with my asthma.
Something lumpy, covered with pyjama.

It took up so much bed, that pallid barrier!
Would it have mattered if we rolled together?
She wouldn't like it, said we slept much sounder.
We never dragged it out; I would remember.

I marked no face on it. The old dictator
Wouldn't let me. Would we have known it better?
Sometimes at night it rises up to chide me,
A puffy worm with a face I never painted,
That slept between. Now we are separated,
My brother dead, it wants to lie beside me.

AT THE CROSS KEYS

Some clutching drinkers slid them, some would slap
Down their dominoes at the Cross Keys
To which I pushed my uncle's wheelchair. Up
Beacon Hill was steep enough to please
A boy no end. What did I have to sup?
No, not the punning porter. Each of those
Evenings was full of huddled dominoes
Loomed over by that gaitered marvel Mr
Blacklock the publican, a gamekeeper.

Memory's taproom leaves no taste but shows
A swarthy man with the perfect name. I'd seen
Blackcocks in bird books; and he must have been
Old enough for flintlocks, muzzle-loaders.

A Booth's for uncle, bravest of brave soldiers.

DIADEMAS EXTRA

My uncle tapped the end of his fag on the lid
Of his silver case initialled AA and curved
To fit his pocket. Like Wyndham Lewis he had
An ashtray on a tube beside his chair
He pressed to make his ashes disappear.
I never saw him smoking a cigar.

He served with the Argylls and not the Gunners
But must have heard the bangs if not the rumours
Of Lewis's battery. One of uncle's treasures
Was a huge cigar in a mahogany box
With sliding lid. What kind of soldier smokes
A thing like that? I wondered. Each year I'd fix
My nail in the lid, slide it away and find
The silver shell, read on the lid and band
DIADEMAS EXTRA, likely to explode.

I longed to see him put his match to it,
To be given the empty box for the sake of the slide.

THE BUSTARDS

Though they were the colour of her bottled froth
My aunt hated the bustards, but loved to mention
The thud of fat bodies on her cheek and pillow,
Their low buzz, with a shudder. But, I would tell her,
They were the flies for trout in the dusk.

As I waited with trout for my uncle
The barn owls would float by the bus stop,
Without a sound, I told her. Now they are ghosts.
I know I looked at them living, though ghostly.
Do the bustards still drum on the window?

THE STATIONMASTER

Stationary, stationary, said
The stationmaster. How long I have hated
The word or half of it so often repeated,
Steamed and hissed and squirted in my head
And out of it! How I have envied the drivers,
The pigeons flapping and bubbling in their baskets,
The smutty firemen, the leavers, the arrivers,
Have wanted to follow the shine along the line,
To leave the porter whistling his silly song,
The signals, the points, the buffers, the clatter, the clang,
The gravelled water's dribble and drip
From the elephant's trunk of the floppy pipe,
The labelled mailbags sure of their destination,
The station, the station, the stationary station.

SMOKY SAILOR

Throwing a fag away as he boarded the bus
A grizzle-bearded wag with a white stick
He did not need except to swing or poke
Showed us two hundred fags, the wrong gift
For an old sailor hoping to give up smoke.

'Your friend is killing you,' a fat
Little woman said. He didn't respond to that.
I dared not look at him in case he put
His glittering eye on me to draw me out:
Some nautical bores like to eviscerate.

He picked on the son of a fisherman from Barbados,
Had been to the island many times and told us
What fish the fisherman must have caught,
But the only word I caught was shark:
He seemed to be certain of shark.

He turned from the curly boy to a thinning chap
Who could not tell by the peak which baseball cap
He had put on that day
And took it off to see that it said MAINE,
Where the most snub nose I've seen had often been.

'New England' he said. Did his finger remember the map,
Cape Cod? The man in the baseball cap
Was uncertain about New England and had to admit
He had narrowly missed his service and doing his bit
In khaki or blue for Old England.

'C'est la guerre: C'est la vie!' said the sailor and sang
'Sussex by the Sea'. 'I know that song'
Said the little fat woman, who had not sung along.
(Would she rather sit or lie
Than stand or fall for Sussex by the sea?)

A man came to the front as he reached his stop
And turned to give a look to the old show-off,
A shaven-headed, big-nosed, killing look.
At Treasure Island skull and crossbones flapped
At clambering shrimps; skull scowled at the old shellback.

THE COALMAN

This dust and I have been here much too long,
But not so long as the stone face on the wall
Just round the corner, grinning at the Black Bull,
Its big gob wide, but even more like mine
The cheek, eye socket, nose, unwashably smudged.
I know they laugh as I pass underneath
Sometimes on foot but mostly in my truck
With nylon sacks, each fifty kilograms.
I can't complain – the Black Bull buys my coal
And keeps a roaring blaze this chilly April
In a proper hearth with irons and polished scuttle
For all the drinkers turned out clean
And snobbishly despite crude ways and smut.
No point in dressing up to weigh the stuff
Or even to write the bills. Dust everywhere.
My leather jerkin softens most of the lumps,
Over an old wool jersey: no one knows
The original colours and I've forgotten too.
The trousers were once camouflage, still are,
Make me less visible among my stacks.
Coal's not much thought about by Silversuit
Who toddles from the Bull to his silver car.
One day I'll pull his top-pocket hanky out
And spit on it and wipe my face with it.
Even the huge girls fancy their fat chances.
There's one…. You must have seen those thighs, that bum!
I'll pat my palm print on her pig-pink pants
If only because they are pink and more than once
I've caught a glimpse and thought she'd nothing on.

TWO GUIDES

Shall we compare our guide, with his professional boots,
Who has forbidden trainers on the slopes,
Who has his daily goggled swim in the hotel pool,
Who in his previous life was a health and safety man,
With one who takes straw sandals off and strips
Naked and suddenly leaps
Head first into a black deep swirling current between rocks
And five minutes later reappears, and clambering out
Lays a sea-snail and an enormous shrimp at Lafcadio's feet?

There is a form on which to make our complaint.

HESITATION

Fashioned of copper or bronze
By a Pre-Raphaelite artificer,
The door-knocker of Sir Edmund Gosse
Had to be contemplated before it was knocked.

A mermaid precursor of Art Nouveau
Or a young lady entangled with a dolphin
Had been presented by a female admirer
And hammered from an ashtray for the important function.

DISSATISFIED JACK

Call this a dinner?
I call it a snack.
You eat like a bird
Said matter-of-fact Jack.

This place is a shambles:
Every wall has a crack.
I was cracked to come here
Said matter-of-fact Jack.

Did you learn how to cook
At school, so far back?
It doesn't look likely
Said matter-of-fact Jack.

I've lost thirteen pounds.
My pants have gone slack;
And it's not the elastic
Said mummy's boy Jack.

Why don't we have carpets
To soften your clack?
Why don't you wear thong things
More often? said Jack.

Whenever I want it
You are stiff as a rack,
A rack with no netting
Said randified Jack.

Those sexy net stockings,
The bargain, the pack,
And the black suspenders?
Did they walk? said Jack.

If you must have the truth,
Said Jill, the brass tack
Itself, this suspender
Can dangle a Jack,

So put your fat neck in.
I'll pull down the slack
That hangs in the pants
Of matter-of-fact Jack.

A USEFUL MEETING

I told my friend the date of the next
Meeting at Plumpton knowing he
Wasn't curious in the least,
Didn't think I liked the races.
Was it a joke he didn't see?

I saw the notice from the train.
I knew he thought my tastes suspicious,
Suggestive of concealed disgraces.
He'd been in wait for any chances
Never to speak to me again.

REMEMBERING W PRICE TURNER

The least, he said, of the Gregory Fellers,
I only read one of his thrullers
And found and read his first book lastly;
And now I discover Bill's favourite whisky
Blinking at me with its white letters,
One of the less conspicuous offers.
He brought me some in a medicine bottle
With an inscribed and personal label.
His strict avoidance of the sentimental
Would have discouraged its retention.
Empty, it would have wanted filling
With more of the same, the gurgle calling
Him back to visit the land of the living
With more to spend, at least a pension;
And teeth. How lost? He didn't mention.

Who still considers his Flying Corset,
Binocular bloomers and striving onion,
His Kilroy, going unrecorded?
He left no room or time to fatten.
I'm sad he seems to be forgotten
In Scotland, but some of his women
Including his 'hat trick of mothers and daughters'
Must remember the tough wee charmer
Who coaxed with verses on green paper.
One stopped the night with him and brought her
Little pamphlet. I've lost it somewhere.
'A better poet than you,' he said,
A protégée. Beyond protection
Did she progress from the single section?
They didn't need a double bed.

FULL MOON AT ST SEINE L'ABBAYE, 1906

Have you the moon too in England?
She asked Will Rothenstein
Who was one to tell her the truth
But feel sad at the consequence,
The disappointment it brought,
And one to have thought of the joke
He could tell to Max and to Craig:
That a doctor's daughter could think
England had no such light.
To her the sky over ruined
Cloisters and baths, over France,
Was France, the country of cheese,
Where castles belonged to the sad
And reduced sometimes, where she
Might still fail to believe
The moon could shine so far
And not be particular.

MAX BEERBOHM AND THE LARK

Said Florence B, What is that bird
Singing against the blue so loud?

It is a skylark, said wee Will;
How could you not have known that trill?

But Max has never heard a lark!
He must be told. We must go back.

Max put on gloves and overcoat
And made quite certain he looked right

To meet the lark he had not heard
But was too late to hear the bird.

Another day I hope! said Will
– The Rothenstein not known as Bill.

FASTIDIOUS SMITH

Jonathan Smith is in his grave.
Nobody there to give him a shave.
Jonathan Smith was a very close shaver,
Smoothed his face with a plated razor,
Cut his nails with golden clippers.
No nostril hair survived his nippers.
Jonathan Smith can do nothing about
Horny nails and bristles that sprout.
He can't tell if his beard is black
Or white nor can he pull it back
Into his chin and neck and cheeks
Nor count the hours and days and weeks.
However hard he tries he fails
Even to chew his fingernails
And he suspects his toenails could
Chisel their way through coffin wood.
Says Jonathan Smith, Can I be dead
With all this growth around my head?
Why can't some hair grow on my back
To give some comfort my old bones lack?
How long will he argue about the date
Of death carved on his polished slate?
Says Jonathan Smith, If I can't shave
My beard will grow out of my grave
And gravediggers will clean their boots
On bundles of my hairy roots.
But no one hears poor Jonathan
Now they are sure he's dead and gone.

PIRATE PENCIL

Red black and white my pirate pencil,
Dropped from a bag or bum-slung satchel.
Bone bow ties and grins too cheerful.

Bone-brittle wood, no scent of cedar.
Bicorne hat and red bandana.
What will it write and smudge with rubber?

More to divert my lipless friend
From a black-patched socket not to mend?
He'll stop my nonsense in the end.

Buccaneer heads and one half head
In blood or midnight, skulls round dead
Pine and the words in a slug of lead.

FATSHIRT'S PRESCRIPTION

Who should I meet but Fred Fatshirt down for the day!
His felt pen battery of coloured rockets
Was loaded and ready to launch from jacket pockets.
His snazzy tie and white belly gave him away.
Dried up, I didn't meet him with my rubber
And blunted pencil to aggravate his blubber.

He prescribed a shed, decrepit, spiders and shatter,
The light of a filthy window, an old wife
To help, mislay the key. (Fatshirt in the gloom
With cobwebs was hard to imagine. He needed room.)
It needed a hole so magpies could squeak at the squatter.

Not far, I said, to go right through the roof.
I'll catch a spark and blaze if I can fly
Your futurist flag, your flash Fred Fatshirt tie.

KING UBU'S BATH

(After Alfred Jarry)

Rampant silver on field of sinople, dragon
Blistered with dribbling sunlight, the bloated Vistula.
There stomps the King of Poland, ex-King of Aragon
Stripped off for his bath, formidable clodhopper.

Dozen dumped into one, pear-shaped paragon,
His fat shudders at his tread, earth under
His puffing; his Patagonian toe snags on
The sharp rim of a rut and shreds a slipper.

Covered with belly he goes as with a shield.
Illustrious redundancy of arse
Strains common underpants beyond their power.

Porkraitured there in his most natural gold
Pigment, a redskin on the warpath, horse
At full stretch, confronts the Eiffel Tower.

THE JUGGLER

How I wanted to be him, the juggler, the painted man!
I would stand not too close, not close enough for him
To notice my fascination, not wanting to disturb
His intense and easy concentration.
                              Then one morning
One of his balls, of the unbouncing kind,
Landed on the high windowsill of the bank and stayed,
And he tossed up another to dislodge it, and could not,
And again and again until it stopped beside the other,
And another and another, and now I do not remember
How many grey balls waited in a rebellious line
Of all his humorous balls like a small boy's mud bombs
Along the windowsill of the bank.
                              And so the juggler
Had to go in the bank, to jump the queue , to ask not for money
– Of which he had some if not plenty in a box or a hat,
His painted box or patchy hat, I do not remember –
But for his balls from their safe deposit,
His pierrot face his proof of ownership.
How could he demonstrate without his balls?

DOBBO THE ROOFMAN

We waited until the gulls and their black-beaked squealers
Had flown off and their stamping had stopped
As we didn't think they would take to Dobbo the Roofman
And the destruction of their property.

It was just swish swish swish
At the other house I just did
Said Dobbo the Roofman swinging his arm.
I knew it wouldn't be easy, I said.

That apple hit me on the head.
It must have had a good aim,
Said Dobbo the Roofman as he knocked
And swung the branch with his longest ladder.

Two three-ply boards with blobs of paint disposed
According to the Laws of Chance were the works of Dobbo
    the Roofman.
Two rungs stopped them falling with him into the sunroom
When he stood on them in his huge soft boots.

It gets thinner and thinner, this plastic,
Said Dobbo the Roofman,
And they don't stick the ends on with mastic.
The best thing to use, he said, shaking his big red rag, is a rag.

Stand on the ladder and hold this
In case I slide off the end. A good thing it's dry
Said Dobbo the Roofman. I stood where he could hit me
With a shower of black bits to prove he was doing the job.

You are up there just like Eric Gill
Carving Ariel on Broadcasting House, I said,
Looking up to Dobbo the Roofman.
They could see his balls, but he wasn't wearing your shorts.

DRILL INSTRUCTOR'S DINNER

Do you remember the pseudo guardsman's peak,
Elft, 'ight and the short sharp shuffle
Of the awful corporal, blue?

Yes, and when I do
I wonder what became of him after kerfuffle.
Did he bawl at a wife and fork? stabbed bubble? burnt squeak?

A FRECKLED VISITOR

When mother invited her freckled young friend from the nuthouse
To stay a few nights with us it wasn't the freckles
That put me off, nor was it maniacal laughter,
Nor did it matter
That her husband had wriggled away to the hands of another.

We sat before bed on the linen box together
At her command. I had a scatter of freckles
In most places too. It was her relentless tickles
That maddened and gave me no desire to discover
How freckled she was, how friendly not only to mother,
Who might have thought a mingling, a cohabitation,
A bed with ruckles,
Would ease my own as well as her condition.

RHYME OF THE SCRIBBLER'S MOTHER

I hope some nasty piece of work
    Will complicate his legs
And twist him like a wonky fork
    Or slipping on his segs

He'll bite a wall of lumpy grit
    And break his grinning teeth
Or tomahawks chop off a bit
    Of head and rusty growth.

(Now that I think of it he might
    Like the exotic thrill.
An ordinary axe is right
    To do the job as well.

Less chance to swank.) He thinks he's it
    For writing lines that rhyme
And daubing hardboard while I knit
    – When scribbling gives him time.

He's making faces at himself,
    Self Portrait with Loose Screw,
Oil slashed on with school dinner knife,
    Fils of Le Père Bouju,

That cove he showed me, by Vlaminck,
    His pipe less smoked than chewed,
A rotten salad of a clock.
    His pop was not so crude.

He's tapping on pop's portable
    Before he learns to type.
His stuff might be acceptable
    In magazines of tripe.

He told me that at ten past nine
    He knew the way to spell.
He mixes words with turpentine
    And gulps the loathsome smell,

But when he's hunched and scribbling
    And does not let me see
He's mouthing and he's dribbling,
    Grotesquifying me.

If I can damn him hard enough
    He'll meet a sticky end
Or scratch his wordy head right off
    In sawdust for the wind.

He says he'll go to London town
    Where people know what's what.
Too perspicacious for the clown
    They're sure to let him rot.

EPISODE AT HALIFAX

She scowled at mangle's lippy grin,
Green paint on rusty iron legs.
Cold concrete scratched across her segs.
She made the spitting rubber spin.
Then suddenly to break its door
The coal burst through. The catch shot out
And through the coalhole throwing more
– Though it was not his pout that flung –
She saw the coalman's smudgy pout,
Until he shut it with a clang
And banged the back door with the bill
– A bill not hard enough to bang.
She cursed the door and its collapse
Up on the hill at Halifax.
She kicked the coal and climbed the steps
And spanked him on the smutty stubble
To thank him for his toil and trouble
– A rubbery and suddy clout –
And then returned to turn the man-
gle handle, mangle on until
The coal decided to back out.

YOUNG BEGGAR IN ANDALUSIA

(After Valery Larbaud)

Between Cordoba and Seville
Is a little station where the express to the south
Stops for no apparent reason.
In vain the traveller looks round for a village
Beyond this little station sleeping under eucalyptus.
He sees only the Andalusian country green and golden.
But across the other line, facing him,
Is a little hut of blackened branches and earth.
And at the sound of a train a ragged gang of urchins comes out of it.
The older sister leads, comes close to the edge of the platform,
And, without a word, but smiling,
She dances for a few coppers.
Her feet are black with the dust;
Her dark and filthy face is without any beauty;
She dances, and through the wide holes in her cinder-coloured skirt
One can see the naked wriggle of her skinny thighs
And the rolling of her little sallow belly;
At which many a gentleman sniggers
In the cigar scent of the dining car.

IN ROTTERDAM

(After Valery Larbaud)

One morning, in Rotterdam, on one of the quays
(It was the 18th of September 1900, towards eight o'clock),
I noticed two young girls returning to their apartments;
And in front of the big iron bridges they said good-bye,
Their directions not being the same.
They embraced tenderly, their hands trembling
Wanting and not wanting to separate; their mouths
Sadly withdrawn, soon to be brought close again
As their transfixed eyes contemplated each other…
Then they held themselves for a long moment together,
Stood immobile in the general bustle,
As the tugs boomed on the river,
And the trains rattled and whistled on the iron bridges.

BY THE FISHERMAN'S HUT

(after Heine)

We sat by the fisherman's hut
And all looked out to sea;
The fog came down and soon
Was thick as a mermaid's knee.

It wrapped around the lighthouse
Soon after it showed a light,
And a ship was lost in the distance
But another one came in sight.

We spoke of storms and shipwreck
And the mariner's risky life
Between the sea and the sky,
Temptation and the wife.

We spoke of the North and West,
Of the South and tropical coasts,
Of strange and horrible habits,
Baubles and teeth and boasts,

Of the sickly pong of the Ganges,
Of lanterns flames and glooms,
Of the silent graceful people,
Their lotus flowers and tombs.

In Lapland the people are dirty,
Flat-headed, wide-gobbed and small;
They squat by the fire and bake codfish
And croak and giggle and brawl.

In England the men are solemn
And pickle their snouts in ale.
In France they would rather skewer
Than hear the nightingale.

The girls gave all their attention
 But had next to nothing to say,
And in the fog and darkness
The ship had slipped away.

THE SHEPHERDS

(After Gabriele D'Annunzio)

September, restless month of migration.
In the Abruzzi my shepherds are leaving;
driving their flocks in a seaward direction
they descend to the boisterous Adriatic,
green as their pastures, their home in the mountains.

Deeply they drank from rustic fountains,
enough for the well-loved taste to comfort
homesick hearts and act as a charm
so thirst on the journey can work no harm.
Each carries a fresh-cut hazel cane.

And they take the old drovers' paths to the plain,
tracing, as if by a silent river
of grass, the steps of the early fathers.
O voice of the one who before any other
senses the glittering shuddering reaches!

Now by the shore the long flock stretches,
making its way through a changeless air
through which the light of the sun dyes blond
the living wool till it looks like the sand.
Hoof-tread of sheep, the soft splash of the sea.

Ah, with my shepherds, there I should be!

CLARA GREYLEES

(After Francis Jammes)

I love in times past Clara Greylees
Who was a pupil at old boarding schools,
Who walked in warm dusks under the may trees
And read defunct periodicals.

I love her only, feel over my heart
Her white breast's illuminated blue.
Where is she? How could such joy depart?
Into her bright room branches grew.

Who knows? Perhaps she is living still
– Or perhaps we were both already dead.
In her courtyard dead leaves scuffed in a chill
Wind to tell us summers had fled.

Think back! The peacock feathers used to swank
By seashells, in the vase with the long neck.
We heard how there had been a shipwreck;
We used to call Newfoundland the Bank.

Come back, come back, O Clara Greylees:
Let us love again if you exist.
The old garden has the old tulips.
Come back naked O Clara Greylees.

THE FOUNTAIN GIRL

(After Max Jacob)

I have dreamed in the night of the fountain girl
in a silk gown as bright as the sea
and I married to her, but our child was blind.

One day more than twenty monks passed on the river.
Such beautiful songs they sang
for one who rose from the dead
for the honour of the nailed God.

'Take me with you in your boat.
I shall play the harp like our Lord Abbot!
You will teach me music.'

In the cloister my mother said:
'Give back my son
the mainstay of the family!'
– 'Your son is no longer here with us: he is in England
teaching the Prince of Wales to play his instruments.

'He has married the fountain girl
and his blind boy sings melodies of his own making.'

SMOKE

(After Théophile Gautier)

There, in the shade of trees,
A hump-backed cottage;
The roof sags, the wall is
Crumbling, the doorstep mossy.

The window is the mouth
Of this dump, and in cold
Weather the chilled breath
Slips away in a cloud.

From the soul of this wreck,
Lifting the news to God,
A corkscrew of smoke
Twists in a thin blue thread.

THE SNAKE HOLE

(After Théophile Gautier)

Along the wall when sunlight's touching
To warm my sluggish circulation
With cats and dogs and the good-for-nothing
At noon I stretch my exhumation.

I lie with neither dream nor thought,
A loafer down to his last penny,
Confront my life, three-quarters spent,
Old man whose life was always empty.

Nothing to love me, no one to love,
My wasted soul forsakes my body;
Within myself I carry my grave;
I am more dead than the dead already.

When the sun has gone behind a cloud
Into my hole I drag myself back,
Into the dark my sorrows provide
Withdraw again as cold as a snake.

HER SHOES

Beside his wife's clodged boots, cobwebs, sucked flies,
A pair of high-heeled shoes stood in the porch,
Black, patent leather, lined with yellow silk,
Like gaping fledglings demanding to be fed.
They were not cracked enough for mother's shoes.

Whose then?... He'd keep them, but they'd have to starve
Pressed mouth to mouth in tissue in a box
Or tight in a bag, heels out, until she came
To knucklebone and nosebone on the door,
To show her widest smile and wormy toes.